MADE WITH LOVE

BY

_____

_____

I love when you

You taught me
how to

_____

_____

_____

_____

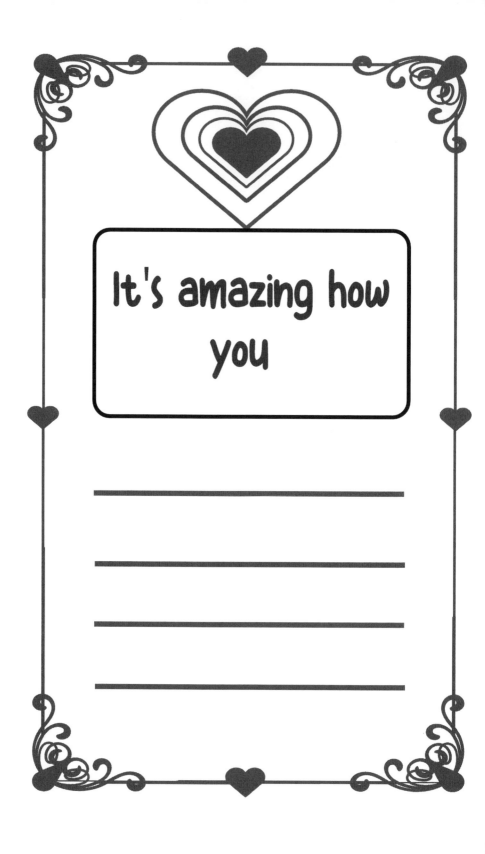

It's amazing how you

I love your

You are good at

Funniest thing you
do is

You are a perfect

You always have
time to

I love you because

You give me the best

You work hard at

I'm impressed by your

You motivate me to

Iam so happy you made me

It makes me smile when

_____

_____

_____

_____

I'm proud to say you are

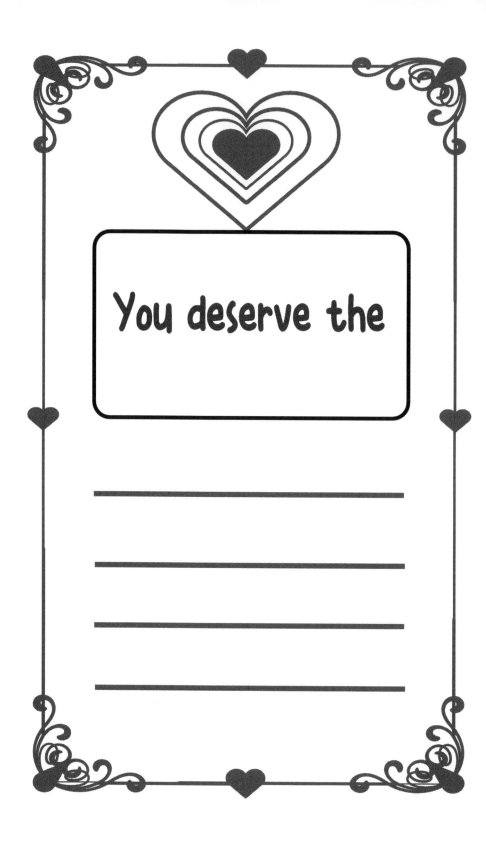

You deserve the

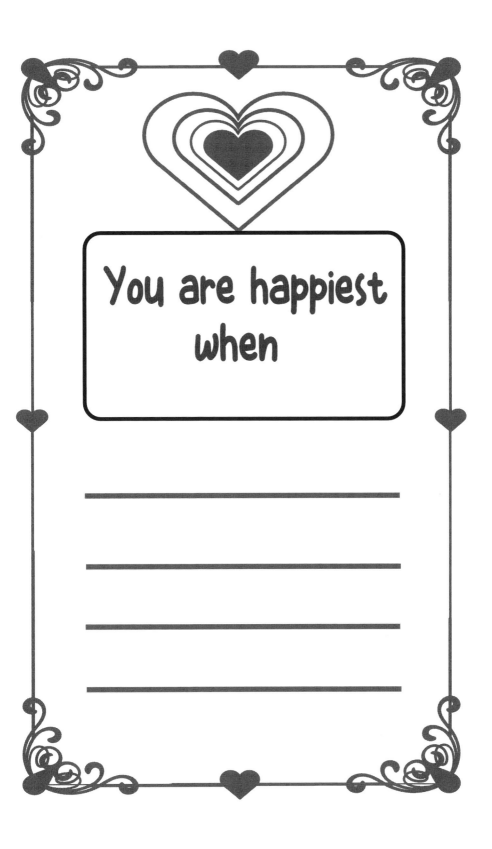

You are happiest when

I love how you
never

I love you because

You were right about

I love you more than

I love how you always

You made me feel
special when

I will always be grateful for your

_____

_____

_____

_____

A time we've laughed the hardest was

You could win a talent show with your

I want you to know that you are

I love the pleasure
you take in

I love when you
tell stories about

We always have
the best time
when we

Best thing about
your job is

I love getting your advice on

Thanks for
encouraging me to

_____

_____

_____

_____

I love your
attitude towards

I admire your dedication to

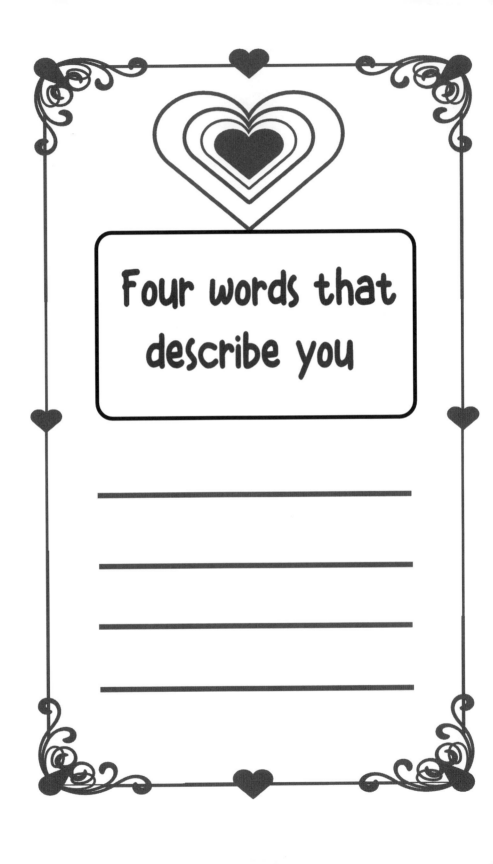

Four words that describe you

_____

_____

_____

_____

I love how you
always say

This is what we have in common

Your funniest joke was

You gave me the courage to

You are special to me because

I never get tired of your

My favorite thing about you is

I value your
advice about

Our favorite thing
to do is

You will always be my

I wish we have more time to

I love how you

I can't forget when

I smile when you

I love it when you

I like when you call me

You make me
laugh when

I wish i have your

Thankyou for

You always help
me to

We have so much
fun when

You inspire me to

You like to

Made in the USA
Monee, IL
04 May 2022

95929670R00037